Testimonials

Pastor Rob and Karen Longmire
Campus pastors at Destiny Worship Center, Freeport, Florida

In 2nd Corinthians 12:9 says, "My grace is sufficient for you, for my strength is made perfect in weakness." On May 1, 2013, that all *sufficient* became a life force for Ivette Vasquez. We would see this play out in our front-row seat to this tragedy surrounded by grace. We are honored and privileged to have walked alongside Ivette as she faced the greatest heartbreak of a mother.

We watched as she stood strong in her faith in Jesus Christ through the countless negative reports from medical staff for her husband. We are forever changed by everything we saw God do during that unimaginable tragedy and by the strength of the woman walking it out.

We will cherish our times driving to and from the hospital and doctors' appointments. We would listen as Ivette shared with us the incredible revelations and encouragement she received from God and memories of Abigail. Our daughter Bethany was a close friend of Abigail's, and her life was touched and encouraged by having known sweet Abigail.

We love you, Ivette, and always will. There are people in your life for a season and others for a lifetime. Ivette and her family are lifetime people to our family. This book will be an encouragement to all who read it!

Linda Huber
My best friend for over ten years

Ivette is the most courageous person I know. Her steadfast trust in the Lord and His goodness in the face of tragedy and heartache has been a testimony of great faith to me and to so many others.

Being friends with Ivette, Johnny, and their family has given me the privilege of experiencing life with them during some of their most difficult days but also days of great victory!

I'm continually amazed by the strength that rises up in Ivette when she is confronted with challenges and circumstances beyond her control. I love that she chooses to cling to the Lord and His promises to her and her family.

I can't wait to see all that God has put in her heart come to fruition. She'll tell you this herself: "What the enemy meant for evil, God meant for good."

Candy Bertrand
My friend for over ten years and church group leader

For more than ten years, I have had the privilege and honor to know Ivette, as well as have a beautiful friendship with her. What a remarkable experience it has been to see Ivette's light shine and witness her strong commitment to the Lord as she walked through such adversity. As you read her story, I believe you will see these wonderful things also.

Melissa D'Anouy
My friend for over ten years and counselor
The Kitchen Table Counseling & Life Coaching Services, Lafayette, Louisiana

Ivette is a woman of great strength. I was privileged to be one of the many women that came alongside her during this season of great loss and tragedy in her family. She was such an example of faith that not only blessed me but encouraged and challenged me in my own walk with Christ! There are a few women that I know that have walked this road the way she has—real, transparent, but strong in the Lord. She never wavered; in her darkest night, she kept her eyes and heart fixed on Jesus!

Beauty in the Storm

Finding Peace in Life's Unforeseen Tragedy

Ivette Vasquez

WestBow Press
A DIVISION OF THOMAS NELSON
& ZONDERVAN

Copyright © 2016 Ivette Vasquez.

All rights reserved. No part of this book may be used or reproduced by any means, graphic, electronic, or mechanical, including photocopying, recording, taping or by any information storage retrieval system without the written permission of the author except in the case of brief quotations embodied in critical articles and reviews.

WestBow Press books may be ordered through booksellers or by contacting:

WestBow Press
A Division of Thomas Nelson & Zondervan
1663 Liberty Drive
Bloomington, IN 47403
www.westbowpress.com
1 (866) 928-1240

Because of the dynamic nature of the Internet, any web addresses or links contained in this book may have changed since publication and may no longer be valid. The views expressed in this work are solely those of the author and do not necessarily reflect the views of the publisher, and the publisher hereby disclaims any responsibility for them.

Any people depicted in stock imagery provided by Thinkstock are models, and such images are being used for illustrative purposes only.
Certain stock imagery © Thinkstock.

ISBN: 978-1-5127-6959-3 (sc)
ISBN: 978-1-5127-6960-9 (hc)
ISBN: 978-1-5127-6958-6 (e)

Library of Congress Control Number: 2016921039

Print information available on the last page.

WestBow Press rev. date: 12/27/2016

Contents

Testimonials i
A Note from Mom vii
Introduction ix
Chapter 1 My Family 1
Chapter 2 Upside Down 13
Chapter 3 Letting Go 25
Chapter 4 New Normal 35
Chapter 5 Let's Fight 43
Chapter 6 Rebuild 57
Chapter 7 Be Still 69
Abigail's Poem 85
Family Photos 87
Afterword 93
Acknowledgments 95
Please Share 97

A Note from Mom

Dear Abigail,

We often spoke about you being the author in the family. You wanted to write so many books and travel the world. Thank you for trusting in me enough to pass your baton down to me. We miss you very much. Every day we see your picture and speak of you. You are the constant thread that passes through the fabric of our thoughts.

Thank you for loving the Lord with all your heart. When I heard about your last words, it gave me joy knowing how much you loved the Lord. As a mom, it gives me great peace knowing we will see each other again. This is far more important than anything I will ever do in my life. This hope gives me the strength I need daily to keep moving forward.

We are all so happy that you are in heaven with the Father. He loved you first, then entrusted you to us. Now He has called you home. Our goal is to spend eternity in heaven. Thank you for the encouragement in my dreams and in my safe place. You left a great legacy, and because of it, your family is blessed. You left an amazing story for your sibling to see as an example and share.

Because of all that's happened to our family, we have a new perspective of life. It's beautiful now, and things are simple. We all love you very much and remember you with smiles. I still remember what you would tell me: "Life is beautiful, Mami; dress accordingly." The most important thing is that I will see you again. This is not the end.

Love,

Mami

Introduction

This book is my story about His glory. I had tragedy hit my home, but in my darkest hour, I ran to my heavenly Father. He has and continues to restore my family. There is so much that happened to my family that I can't possibly write everything in one book. God has blessed us tremendously.

My husband and I prayed so much for this book. We talked and planned. The question that kept popping up was, what do you want this book to do? The answer was to touch many lives. We want it to be an evangelistic book to testify of how great is our God. We want people to know that with God, all things are possible. Even in your darkest hour, the Father is there to make it all turn around for your good for those who love Him. We have to praise God in good and bad times. So, that's what we did. We wrote an outline of each chapter, only keeping the most important details.

This will be my foundation for my other books that will follow. We will have a book all about Abigail where we will discuss more details, dreams, and visions. There will be more to follow, but this is the rock of them all. I hope our story will touch you. We pray that you will be encouraged and that you will want to share with others our story. There are many people that need Jesus, and this can be a tool just for that.

I want to thank everyone in our family, our spiritual family, friends, and the community for stepping out and covering us with their love. We definitely would not have been able to do everything without you all.

Special thank you to my son Elias, for stepping up and helping me with Dad, his siblings, and the house. To my daughter Zoei, for entertaining us every step of the way. She has taken initiative to help as well with anything that comes up. To my baby boy, Legend, thank you for being the joy in our lives.

Finally, I saved the best for last ... my husband, for being understanding and knowing that we wanted to be the best for him. We had many crazy times, and he always encouraged me that tomorrow will be better. He is an amazing man. He has kept good spirits through this all.

Thank You, Lord, for making all this possible.

Chapter 1

My Family

Her Poem

Weeks passed since my life changed, and I was overwhelmed with emotions. I was looking for my journal to write down my feelings. *I found it.* As I opened it, a piece of paper fell out. It was a poem my daughter Abigail had written for me.

As I read it, I saw it in a different light. It was like she knew. It had prophetic undertones, and it spoke volumes that morning. My husband and I been through many storms before, but this one was the hardest. I knew the day we met that nothing would tear us apart.

Meeting Johnny

In the spring of 1993, Johnny was at his first duty station in Fort Polk, Louisiana. He was in the army like my stepfather. My family lived there for about a year before meeting Johnny at a small country church. My mother taught me to greet new visitors with a blessing. Johnny was new to our church, so I went to greet him. I said, "God bless you."

He replied, "I didn't sneeze."

I didn't think he was funny, but he was cute. He became close with my stepfather and started coming to my home frequently. *Oh, he's sneaky,* I thought. After a while, we started to date and fell in love.

Our relationship was off and on for a couple of years. It wasn't easy, but we were meant to be together. In the fall of 1996, we were married by our pastor, Sidney Morales, at a military chapel. We spent our first two years of marriage in South Korea. It was Johnny's only overseas tour. There we learned to depend on each other and grow together as a couple.

Our Growing Family

Shortly after we returned to the States, I found out I was expecting my first child. We were excited about this chapter in our life. It wasn't easy to find out the gender of our baby. Every time we had an ultrasound visit, the doctor couldn't tell.

One day, we went in for a routine checkup close to my due date. To our surprise, I was told it was time to deliver to prevent complications. Johnny was by my side for the several hours of labor. After I gave birth, I asked, "Is it a boy or a girl?"

The doctor replied, "It's a girl."

Johnny named her Abigail, which in Hebrew means *father's joy*, because she would bring her daddy much joy. Immediately, Johnny raised her and dedicated her to the Lord.

Four years later, Elias was born. Finally, it was great to have a son added to our family! God had answered my prayer; I had a little man running around the house. I called him my preacher. Abigail was so excited to have a little brother as a playmate. We felt blessed to have a girl and a boy. "Is this it?" we asked.

We thought we were done, but our family continued to grow five years later when Zoeí joined the crew. She added excitement to our lives. *If only I could bottle her energy!* Johnny said, "Zoeí! Life as God gives it." (This is the meaning of her name.) He had picked her name out two years before she was born.

Five years later, Legend came when we needed him the most. He was unexpected, but God knew best. God answered Elias's prayer for a little brother to be a tougher playmate. Legend fit the bill for roughhousing, and Elias had the bruises to prove it. But you would never know it because Legend has always been a sweetheart. He brought joy to us in our darkest time.

This is the Vasquez crew.

Our Faith

Throughout our family years, we have always been active in our Christian faith at home and at church. My husband was a deacon, youth pastor, worship leader, choir member, church administrator, and volunteer children's pastor. I assisted my husband in all the roles he had taken. I also was part of the staff doing administration for different ministries.

Like every family, we had our fights, tears, and heartaches. In the end, they brought us forgiveness, joy, and strength. We taught our children to be true to who they are and always put God first.

Moving to the City

After Johnny left the army, we bought our first house in a nearby small town called Rosepine. It was quiet country living. While living in our first home, Johnny earned two associate's degrees: one in office systems and one in accounting.

For many years, Pastor Sidney was our mentor and friend. He asked Johnny to join him in Lafayette to help in a Hispanic church he'd started. Johnny felt it was time for us to move and use his skills in the ministry.

In the spring of 2002, we moved to Lafayette to start a new chapter in our life. Too bad our home couldn't make the trip with us. I loved our little house. This was where Abigail grew into a beautiful young girl. But we were excited to be in the ministry. Honestly, I was looking for more city than country. Lafayette has the right mixture of both.

Our Savior's Church

About three years later, Johnny felt it was time to join Our Savior's Church (OSC). We spoke to Pastor Sidney about our feelings, and he gave us his blessing. Before leaving, Johnny spoke to the congregation to say our good-byes. We cried and hugged many of them. Still today, we keep in contact with Pastor Sidney as a mentor and friend.

In the fall of 2004, we went to our first official service at OSC. We had attended as visitors before, but now this would be our new church. Pastor Jacob Aranza was the senior pastor at OSC. His weekly messages were both practical and inspiring. We loved the atmosphere and the people. *It felt like home.*

My children grew up loving our spiritual family and friends. At first, we went with the flow and learned how they operated. We knew the greatest blessing about going to church was serving others. In time, we would move from the pews into action.

At the time, there were two campuses for the church. One was in Broussard, and the other was in Lafayette. We were regular attendees at the Lafayette campus, but after a short period, we were asked to volunteer in the children's ministry.

Our reaction was funny because we never considered children's ministry as seriously as the youth ministry. We were used to the teens because of the years we served as youth pastors. They told us it worked the same. We were in for a treat.

We fell in love with OSC children. This would be the place we developed a relationship with Pastor Scott and Lessa Brantingham. God would use this amazing couple in our life in such a big way. They were our leaders and friends. With their guidance, we learned how to be fun and relevant children's pastors.

After a few years, we bought our second home in Breaux Bridge and started to attend the Broussard campus. We were asked to be volunteer pastors at the campus. It was such an honor to serve.

For many years, Johnny worked as an accounting clerk at a construction company. I started to work as administrative assistant in children's ministry after arriving at the Broussard campus. For five years, I loved working on staff at the church. It was amazing to see how my church was committed to excellence in serving our community.

Our Prophecy

Years ago, we were prophesied by a visiting preacher. He told us we would have a testimony that would reach many. We left that service feeling puzzled. We couldn't think of any testimony that would be this impactful. I thought the prophecy was about current events, but it would not come to pass for several years.

After several months in OSC, a visiting pastor and prophet chose to prophesy over us. The prophecy became very important in our life. It spoke about our past, our current situation, and our future. This prophet said that Johnny would have three battles over his destiny where the enemy himself would stand in front of us to impede his progress. The third battle would mark our lives forever in which the Lord would do the impossible for my husband and me.

After the man of God finished, I was in tears. This is important for you to know because you are going to learn about the final battle.

Our Comfort Zone

God has done a great work in our lives during the years we have been at OSC. We have matured spiritually. We have learned that we need other people in our lives. Acquaintances are not enough. We needed to grow and do life together.

Our church's life groups were a big part of us. This was where we developed these relationships. My children love God and the church. This is very important to us. Some families fight to get their kids to church; my children would be mad if we had to miss it.

Our life was comfortable. We planned on fixing up our house because we had family from out of state that would visit and wanted big gatherings at my home. Our kids loved to play outside on the two lots we owned. Everything was looking great. Nothing could go wrong, until it did.

Big Changes

In the fall of 2012, my husband came home from work with dinner and a movie for the family. Everything seemed fine, but in my spirit, I knew something was off. I thought, *What is he not telling me?* I asked, "Is everything okay?"

He gave me that look and didn't reply. *I knew it.*

When we went to our room, he told me he'd lost his job. He was surprised by my reaction. I was actually okay with it. I knew he was no longer happy working there, and it was time for a change. He had spent seven years working, and slowly his spark had been leaving. He needed my support, not my rejection.

The next day, we told our children the big news about how Dad would be home more while looking for work. Abigail at first thought the big news was about me being pregnant. It was funny she said those words because I was feeling weird.

Later that day, we bought a few pregnancy tests—a few because Johnny couldn't believe I was expecting our next child. After the shock, we were excited about our soon-to-be baby. God was up to something good, and in the coming months, we would see it unfold.

Things Were Getting Better

My husband did some odd jobs to keep the family going. He collected unemployment for a while, then started work in the new year as a tax preparer. He worked odd times but made good money. Tax season was winding down, and soon he would be looking for new work.

One evening while driving home from work, a friend who owned a construction company called him about working for him. Johnny met with him to work out the details.

His friend agreed to Johnny's asking pay and hours. This was great news. The income gave us the opportunity to get out of the debt we'd fallen into due to his job loss. He had time to pick up the children from school, helped them with their homework, and cooked dinner. *It was heavenly.*

Every year, we would go on our vacation to SeaWorld. This year was no different because his friend was generous enough to give Johnny a paid vacation. We had such an amazing time as a family. We really needed this break after the stress of finding new work. Everything was getting better again, and I could see Johnny's spark was coming back.

In April 2013, my sister came to visit from Texas to spend Easter with us. We had such a big gathering. I had my three sisters, their husbands, and all my nephews home with us. We had so much fun taking pictures, eating together, and playing family games.

The following weekend after Easter, my mom and her husband came to surprise us from Oklahoma. Elias surprised us in church by deciding to get baptized. It was a blessing to have the family come visit us after not seeing them for a year. God is so good.

Reflection Time

I can see how God was moving during this season. Johnny spent more time with us because of his new job. This gave him a chance to make up all the daddy-daughter dates he'd promised to Abigail.

We eliminated most of our debt.

Abigail wrote a beautiful poem about trees especially for me. This is the same poem I mentioned earlier. Later, she came home with a lovely portrait of a tree. She was so excited to show it to me. She even hung it up on the wall in the living room. The portrait and poem still encourage me today.

We had unexpected visits from our extended family. Usually our visits are planned later in the year, but for no apparent reason, they all came early that year. This gave us a chance be together as a family for one last time before my world was flipped upside down.

Chapter 2

Upside Down

My Last Normal Day

May 1, 2013, was like every other Wednesday morning. In two days, we would leave for a special family trip to the beach for Abigail's fourteenth birthday. Johnny rented a beach house for the weekend to have a precelebration. We would take one of her friends to join us on the trip. Everyone was in high spirits, especially Abigail.

It was my eighth month of pregnancy with Legend, and I wasn't feeling well. I woke up my children to get them started on their morning routine. I came back to my room to get ready, but out of nowhere, Johnny told me to rest because he was taking our children to school. I was super surprised because it was my turn to take them to school. He usually didn't just pass up his sleep-in days. I asked, "Are you sure?"

He said, "Yes, baby, I got this."

I happily jumped back into my bed.

Abigail and Elias got dressed; they made breakfast for themselves and Zoeí. Johnny woke me to lock the door before he left with the children. For some reason, I stared at Abigail as she got into the car. *My goodness, she is so beautiful. I am so proud of her.* This would be the last time I saw my family together.

The Words I Never Wanted to Hear

It was just me and Zoeí at home. She was eating the breakfast that Abigail had made. She was a happy four-year-old. I ended up doing a couple of things around the house. Then I told Zoeí, "I am going to eat cereal this morning." As I was eating, I got the call.

Because of our longtime relationship from children's church, Pastor Scott [Brantingham] was one of our school's emergency contacts. He said, "Ivette, they have been trying to call you about Abigail being at Lafayette General [Hospital], something about her leg."

I replied, "Okay, I am on my way." Ever since I'd dropped my cell phone the night before, it hadn't been working right. I could make calls but only received some calls, and on top of that, I'd lost all my contacts.

Beauty in the Storm

At first, I didn't think anything too bad had happened to Abigail. *Maybe she had a bad fall, and since I couldn't be reached, they took her to the hospital.* I was worried, but I thought everything would be fine. *It can't be too serious.*

As I was getting Zoeí ready to go, I got my second phone call. This time, it was my best friend, Linda Huber; she was also on the school's emergency contact list. She said Elias was at the ER of Our Lady of Lourdes. He was okay, and she was going to head over there. I paused and thought, *what is going on?* I had a knot in my stomach. My heart started to beat really fast. Immediately, I called Johnny, but there was no answer. I left him so many messages about the children's situation.

Finally, I got a third phone call from my sister Delia. She said, "Sayi [my nickname], I got a phone call that the kids didn't make it to school this morning. There's been a car accident. Johnny and EJ [Elias's nickname] are at Our Lady of Lourdes. I am on my way there. You should go see Abigail because she is in another hospital—Lafayette General."

Shifting to Autopilot

I don't even know how I got dressed. Because I'd lost all my contacts, I called Pastor Scott back. I desperately said, "There was an accident. Johnny and the children are in different hospitals. I don't have any contacts. I'm shaking; I can't drive. I need someone to pick me up and take me to Abigail."

He said, "I will take care of everything."

A moment later, he called to say that my friend Christina was coming to get me; she lived very close. I looked at Zoei and thought, *I don't want her to get upset ... I need to keep it together.* I put her [Nintendo] DS, games, and everything she needed in her bag.

Before I knew it, Christina was there. We got in my truck, and she started to drive. She could tell that I was nervous. She was praying while we were driving. I could feel my heart beating and hear every breath I took. I felt numb to the world around me. I could see and hear, but I was somewhere else.

Every second felt like minutes. It seemed to be the longest drive I'd ever had. Still to this day, I wished I'd left on the first call. I could have talked to Abigail while she was alert, before she was prepped and medicated for the operation.

It's Okay to Go

Once we got to the hospital, I had no idea what to expect, but I was hoping for the best. As I walked in the ER of Lafayette General, I was greeted by Pastor Scott and some of my church family. *I'm so glad they are here.* I was a nervous wreck. I was trying

Beauty in the Storm

to keep it together, but my knees were shaking, and my heart was beating fast.

I'm grateful Pastor Scott stood beside me the whole time. The doctor came to say, "Mrs. Vasquez, Abigail suffered several injuries due to the car accident. I am going to attempt to fix what I saw in the MRI. I do not think she will walk again. If she does, we will have to do several operations to get there."

That was it. That was all I could take. I didn't hear another word out of his mouth. His lips were moving, but no sound.

Before they could operate, I was moved to a room to sign a bunch of papers. Soon after, I heard him say, "You can see her now." She was highly medicated and not able to respond. Basically, I could talk to her for my own closure before they operated. I only had a couple of minutes before they took her away. I felt in my spirit to tell her that it was okay if she wanted to go with Jesus.

Our Final Talk

There were nurses and all kinds of people around her ready to go. I got close, and everyone around me faded away. I could sense the Holy Spirit guiding me. I went close to her ear. I said, "Abigail ... Papi, Mami, EJ, and Zoeí love you very much. We are here for you. I know that you are strong. If you want to fight, we are here for you all the way. I also want you to know that Papi and I dedicated your life to Jesus the day you were born. You belong to Him. If you want to go, it's okay ... you belong to Him."

As I kissed her good-bye, suddenly her hand and head moved up toward me. That was the last time she tried to communicate with me. I know that was her way to say, "I hear you, Mom ... I know you are here." I looked up, and everyone in that room was in tears, surprised by her response.

It was time for her to go. I went out to the hall, and when the bed passed by me, she moved her other arm toward me like she knew that I was standing there. Her eyes were always closed, and she didn't make a sound. As they rolled her away, one of the nurses said, "No, Abigail, stay still, sweetie. You have to stay still."

Waiting

Zoei was cared for by my friend Christina. My pastor, Jacob Aranza, took me to the chapel with my little daughter and my friends to wait for the beeper to go off. I was in a daze of prayer and thoughts. *Lord, save my girl. What is happening to Johnny and Elias?* They were at Lourdes, and no one was giving me an update.

As I waited, someone from the other hospital called, "Mrs. Vasquez, Elias is ready to go home." *Thank God.* It was such a relief to know my son was fine. He had been sitting in the front seat next to his dad, and it was a head-on collision.

Months later, one paramedic said, "When we arrived at the scene, we thought by the look of the accident his legs would have been worse with deep lacerations or wouldn't be good at all. The whole dashboard was smashed on top of his legs, but he came out with minor bruises."

For a while, he did limp and experienced headaches, but a couple of days later, he was physically fine. He is one of my miracles and a little hope I needed at this time of my life. Still not a word on Johnny, even though I called several times.

It's Not His Fault

My son was safe with my best friend, Linda. She took him with her boys to get his mind off things. *I hope Abigail is fine. It feels like I've been here for days.*

As I waited in the chapel, the police came to give details on the accident. The officer said that while Johnny was driving on Interstate 10, there was a vehicle driving on the opposite lane that crossed the median and hit my husband's car head-on.

The officer said, "Everyone in the car had their seat belts on, and it wasn't his fault."

It wasn't his fault echoed in my head. I needed to hear that it wasn't my husband fault—more for his sake than anything else.

Knowing you were the cause of harming your children would be unbearable for a parent. Now I could always remind him of those words if he ever started to blame himself. The officer gave me his card for any further questions. Pastor Scott took care of my husband's vehicle and anything the officer needed.

The Beeper Goes Off

The sound was sobering. *The operation is over.* We quickly moved to the waiting area. I wasn't alone; my friends were sitting on each side of me. Zoei was playing with some toys a friend had bought her. My sister Agnes and her husband came for support. I felt strength from everyone, but I was still very nervous.

My mind was everywhere and here at the same time. *Is she okay? Is she going to walk again? When can I take her home?*

The doctor was ready to talk; we went into another room to discuss the operation and how it had gone. Pastor Jacob and his wife waited with me.

Beauty in the Storm

The doctor walked in and started to talk about procedures he'd done during the operation. It was confusing. *I don't understand the doctor's lingo.*

Suddenly, he said, "That's where we lost her."

I said, "Wait ... wha ... what did you say? What do you mean?"

He looked at me and said, "She is dead." He continued to talk about the operation.

Suddenly, time stopped. I was dropped into limbo. I felt lost. It was like someone gutted me. *How am I breathing?* I felt empty inside. It was the worst feeling I had ever experienced. "I don't care about procedures," I said. *I need him to stop talking.* "I know where she is, and I want to see her!" I cried. I braced myself against the chair, looked up, and wailed, "God, You took her! I need You! I need You now!"

In that moment, it was like heaven opened up, and God poured out His grace. He filled me up with peace and strength that never left me, even to this day. I knew even though God took my daughter, there would be no way for me to continue on without Him. Then the doctor replied, "Give me a few minutes to prepare her so you can see her."

Saying Good-Bye

I was surrounded by love when I needed it the most. My sisters and my beautiful spiritual family filled the waiting room. They were there to cry with me, hold me, or just be there with me. I didn't have to face this alone. That is what life is about—sharing our joys and griefs with our loved ones.

Finally, I was called to the back to see Abigail. Everyone came with me. The room was filled with nurses, but all I saw was her. There she was lying down on the operating table wrapped in white sheets. *She looks beautiful. It's like she's sleeping.* I touched her hands and face.

I cried, "Abigail, I love you. I wanted you to meet Legend. I will make sure he knows all about you. I know you are in heaven. You deserve the best. I am proud of you." Those were just a few things I said to her while crying. I said, "I want to hold her like when she was a baby."

The ones who prepared her said, "Of course."

I held her and spoke softly in her ear for the last time. It was like no one else was there.

After I said my piece, I was ready to leave. Pastor Jacob and his wife both kissed Abigail good-bye. Then he said, "Do not worry about anything. I will take care of all the funeral arrangements." I thanked him and left with my friend Karen to check on Johnny.

What Will Happen to Us?

I left my daughter Zoei with my sister. She took Zoei home to play with her cousin. Thoughts filled my head while Karen was driving. *I just left my Abigail.* It was a strange feeling leaving her body at the hospital. *She's not coming home with me.* I was still in shock. *How am I going to tell Johnny and the children?*

We arrived at Our Lady of Lourdes Medical Center. I got to the intensive care unit (ICU) to find more of my church family. *I love my church.* Pastor Jacob and his wife made it there before we did because we made a wrong turn. Pastor Rob was there the whole time waiting to hear about Johnny.

As I was going to see him, I was stopped by his doctor. He said, "Your husband is in critical condition. In this state, he cannot know about his daughter passing away."

The pastors agreed.

Wow, I just left my daughter, and you want me to act like everything is okay. How am I going to do this? God help me. "Okay," I said. *Johnny is in critical condition ... I have to keep it together for him.* I tried to pull myself together, but I needed help.

As I walked into his room, it was like grace was waiting for me at the entrance. I felt put together, peace, and strength. Immediately, I felt in my spirit,

"For him, you have to fight." With Pastor Jacob by my side, I walked over to Johnny. He seemed paralyzed from head to toe. *What is going to happen to my family?*

I saw the desperation in his eyes. Doctors and nurses worked to attach more tubes on him. *I know you're worried.* He couldn't talk, because of the tube down his throat. There were traces of blood on his arms from the wreck. A halo was on his head to keep it immobilized because he'd broken his neck.

He moved his arms a bit to show me what he could do. The nurse told him, "No, Mr. Johnny ... stay still."

Pastor Jacob told him, "Everything will be okay. We are going to take care of your wife and kids. They will not be left alone. All you have to worry about is getting better for your family so you can come back to them."

I looked at Johnny in disbelief. He was in bad condition. He was the leader of our home. *My God, what's going to happen to us?*

Chapter 3

Letting Go

Abigail's Paramedic

Shortly after Abigail's passing, her paramedic wanted to share with me her last moments when I was available to talk. Later, I learned that she was a member of our church. It was comforting to know that Abigail was surrounded by spiritual family in our time of need.

About three months later, we talked about the day of the accident. This is a condensed and carefully worded version of her account.

> *When we arrived at the scene, your husband was being intubated. Elias and Abigail were alert and talking. I was assigned to Abigail's care. She was in the back-passenger side and looked*

fine. I asked if she felt any pain. She replied that there was no feeling in her legs and her stomach hurt a little.

The other paramedics took her out of the car, and I took off her shoes to rub her legs. She couldn't feel her legs. We were going to wait for Elias, but I felt she needed immediate attention. We decided to take her first to the nearest hospital. She didn't seem scared, nor was she crying.

While in the ambulance, I was able to get all her information along with the church she attended. Before we arrived at Lafayette General, she said, "Let me go. Let me die. I will be okay. I'm ready to be with Jesus." She said this three times with peace in her eyes. It blew me away.

In my ten years of experience, I have never had someone this brave in the face of death. It was as if Abigail accepted what was about to happen. I have taken adults to the hospital crying not to let them die. Here I have a teenage girl saying she is okay with dying. It was as if she was in the supernatural. My life will be forever changed by this young lady.

Stories from Others

I was grateful to have spoken to the paramedic. Nurses and other people filled me in on what had happened after Abigail arrived at the ER. This is a summary of the information I received.

> *"She was so peaceful," said one nurse. "The whole time, I was blessed by the way Abigail spoke with manners. She always responded with a Yes, ma'am' or 'No, ma'am.'"*
>
> *When she was surrounded by nurses, Abigail asked, "Do you know Jesus?"*
>
> *They replied, "Yes, baby. Would you like us to pray for you?"*
>
> *She replied, "Not for me; I will be fine. Please pray for my father, my brother, and the rest of my family."*

Hearing about Abigail's faith in her final moments brought me such peace. She was ready to be in the arms of Jesus. One day, I will be reunited with my Lord and daughter. I hope to have her courage when I die.

This brought me to tears because it confirmed my feeling about letting her go. It was the moment before they took her into the OR. I told her, "If you want to go, it's okay ... you belong to Him [Jesus]."

Though she didn't say a word, she said a lot. She was heavily sedated for the surgery. There could be no possible way for her to respond, but she did by her moving her arms toward me. I feel it was her way of saying, "I hear you, Mom." It's beautiful to see God's hand moving behind the scenes.

God's Amazing Grace

I felt God was with me in the waiting room. When I cried out, "God, You took her! I need You! I need You now!" God gave me peace and strength. Whenever I couldn't go on, it was this gift of peace and strength that carried me into healing.

When I saw Abigail after the operation, she looked beautiful. It was like she was asleep. I got to speak my heart to her, to touch her, to kiss her, and to hold her.

This was important for my healing process. Saying good-bye to my daughter changed my life forever. Her legacy will carry us into our destiny.

Golden Birthday

For years, Abigail talked about her "golden birthday." "It's when the day you were born and your age are the same number," she often said. On May 14, 2013, she would have celebrated her fourteenth birthday.

Weeks leading to her birthday, I saw, "My golden birthday! It's going to be my best birthday ever!" written on her calendar. She was so excited. Counting down each day.

Months after the accident while my husband was at the rehab center, I surprised him for his birthday by showing up unexpectedly. He didn't want to celebrate, because Abigail missed her birthday. I reminded him about her calendar and said, "She didn't miss it. She had the best birthday ever with the Lord Jesus."

I continued to tell him about how we did her funeral on her birthday. The church was full of family, spiritual family, friends, and the community. There were teachers, principals, students, and her friends she'd known from kindergarten through eighth grade. She touched many with her kindness, her smile, and her courage to stand for what she believed. This is what made her so special. These words comforted my husband.

The Funeral Was a Celebration

Since it was a celebration, I asked everyone to wear colorful clothing. Some of her friends and church family wore T-shirts with her picture made by my sweet friend Olivia.

Sadly, my husband wasn't there. He was still in ICU, and we waited to tell him anything about Abigail until he was more stable. It was so hard not to have him there by my side. He loved Abigail dearly. I knew he would regret not seeing her one last time in the flesh. It was the closure we all needed.

At first, my son didn't want to see her in the casket. He wasn't ready to say good-bye or to see her lying there lifeless. After thinking about it, he changed his mind. He said, "I've got to do this. If this is the last time I get to see my sister, then I need to do this." It moved me to tears. *That's my brave boy.*

We went together ... Elias, Zoei, and I went to see her for the last time. I could hear my son start to cry. When he saw her, he cried uncontrollably. He loved his big sister.

Zoei responded differently by standing there frozen, looking at Abigail. She was too young to really grasp the moment. She asked to touch her. I told her it would be fine. "Mom, she's cold," she said.

I cried, "Abigail is not there anymore."

Standing with my children, there was a void. *I wish Johnny and Legend were here.* I gave birth just three days before the funeral. Legend was five weeks premature, and he needed to stay in ICU. My one wish would have been for all of us to be together to say good-bye to Abigail.

Still, many came to show their love and respect. Over four hundred people came to the funeral, we played her favorite music, and Pastor Jacob preached a moving message. Over fifty souls accepted the Lord as their savior and became Christians.

Days after the funeral, I received many e-mails from people who'd rededicated their lives to the Lord. Some parents started to attend church again because they found peace knowing their children will learn about the Lord Jesus. God took our sorrow and brought joy to many. Our joy is full knowing her life made a difference.

Her Legacy Lives On

I knew my daughter was a great girl, but I didn't know how much of an impact she'd made in people's lives. During the weeks after her funeral, I received e-mails from teachers and her friends. One teacher told me that she would make her coffee and always have a beautiful smile.

One friend wrote how she'd planned to commit suicide, but Abigail happen to talk to her one night, and she didn't go through with it.

Another girl wrote me a sweet note about the time when they were in elementary school. They were given Halloween color sheets, but they didn't celebrate it. Abigail quickly told her teacher she didn't want to color the sheets because she didn't celebrate Halloween. "I celebrate Harvest Fest, and I don't want to color this witch," she explained. When she heard, Abigail ask for something else to color, it gave her the courage to do the same. Wow, I am one proud mama. I still get emotional thinking about these things.

Abigail was full of life, and she wanted to be the best "her" she could be. That's it! It was her simple message: "To touch the lives of the people in your community, you have to be the best 'you' you can be. I have to be the best 'me' I can ever be."

People who had never met her are inspired by her story. I plan to share more of these stories in my next book. My family and I made it our mission to keep her legacy alive.

Divine Providence

No parent should ever have to bury his or her child. I can see how a parent can be bitter. I wanted to see Abigail grow up and experience all life had to offer. I will not see her fall in love, get married, and have children. I will not get to read the many books she would have written.

Beauty in the Storm

Though I wanted so much for her, Abigail reminded me that God had greater things for her to experience. I couldn't be bitter. Yes, I wish she were still here. Not only was she my daughter, she was my close friend.

Nothing will ever fill this void, but releasing her to God and embracing this pain helped me to move forward. It helps me to see God's hand in the journey of life. She was never mine, but God's child. He entrusted her in my care, and it was time for her to go home. God reminded me of this truth, and it gives me the hope to see her again.

Now, I'm envious of her. She is experiencing her great mansion in heaven with many interesting people from the Bible. Her favorites are Ruth, Esther, and Mary. I could only imagine the joy of her meeting them.

God did a number of things to prepare us for her departure. Our family visited us earlier in the year than usual. In fact, they came weeks and days before the accident.

Johnny caught up with dates with Abigail. He felt guilty for not doing them because of his busy work. With his new job, he was able to catch up. Abigail loved those times.

One provision that stands out the most is the birth of Legend. We thought three children were enough, but God knew this child would be born at the right time.

Since he was a preemie, he didn't come home until a couple of weeks later. He came home on Elias's birthday. "He's the best gift I ever had," said Elias. I'd never taken care of a preemie before, so the hospital gave me all these instructions.

Knowing I had a little man needing me every minute helped me get through each day. If I was sad, it just took one look from his cute little face to make me smile. Elias and Zoei are now the big brother and big sister. They always looked for opportunities to hold him and feed him.

Still today, they try to be his favorite sibling. God provided for us before and during, and God continues to provide long after the accident. There's no way I will ever let Him go.

Chapter 4

New Normal

Entering into a New Season

About two months before Johnny came home, we moved from our country home to a lovely apartment complex within the city limits.

We had to move because we were no longer able to afford the house, and we wanted to be closer to the resources the city provided. It was hard to say good-bye to our house.

Though we lived there for a few short years, we saw Abigail mature into a lovely young lady. We made some great memories of family gatherings and birthday parties. It was the last place I saw my family together. Nevertheless, we moved forward to the new apartment.

I had some ladies come help with packing. Pastor Rob had put a team together to help with the move.

It took only a couple of hours. Everything was pretty much in place. The children and I adjusted pretty quickly because it felt like we were in a resort on vacation. There were two pools for the residents to use, and we used them as often as we could.

Everything was going to work out, and we could see the light at the end of the tunnel. We were not planning on what to do next. The car accident happened, and our life had been on autopilot. I had to put up my hands and say, "Lord, take me where You will; I trust You."

Missing Their Big Sister

About a week after the accident, I told the children about Abigail passing away. Pastor Rob and Karen came for support and to help answer the children's questions. I had no idea how the children would react.

We sat down together and allowed the pastor to share the news with them. I saw disbelief and confusion in their eyes. After the shock wore off, they started to cry. At the time, Zoeí was four, and Elias was nine years old.

They asked questions that made sense for them. With tears, Elias asked, "So, Abigail is not coming home? Who is going to help me with my homework now?"

Zoeí was trying to grasp the idea that her sister was gone. She said, "Abigail is in heaven. I am not going to see her again. Who is going to make me strudels now?"

Elias saw that his little sister felt abandoned. He replied, "Don't worry, Zoeí. I will make your strudels for you." It warmed my heart to see him wanting to pick up the slack.

Abigail was such a big part of their lives. She was an active sibling, always there for her brother and sister. I let the children express their grief. I told them it was okay to cry because crying brings healing. We stopped any activity if someone needed to share how he or she felt. This helped in the grieving process and healing.

Packing Up Was Hard

I had some help packing, but I did most of it on my own. It forced me to clean out Abigail's room much sooner than I'd hoped. My kids and I didn't want to let go of the place where Abigail had spent her last years.

While on the couch thinking of her, I would often imagine her doing the dishes or sitting at her desk smiling at me. We loved our home and dreamed of raising all the children there, but the reality was it was too much to maintain and afford due to the circumstances.

We found the only apartment available that met all our needs, and the church helped us to move in and unpack. Still today, we often drive by the house to rekindle some memories.

My Children's Journey

I made a conscious decision to give time and resources they needed to move forward. I definitely didn't want them angry at God. Quickly, I learned children process grief the way the parents do.

I needed them to know my faith in God helped me to process my pain. They had to understand that home was their place to express their feelings openly, so it was okay to scream, cry, and punch the pillows, to let the pain out to pick yourself back up. We did it together.

Thankfully, I have great friends and professional Christian counselors like Marc and Melissa. They gave me the guidance to rightly steer my children through their grief.

Melissa gave me the encouragement I needed for many of my hurting days. During that season, she sent me a little nugget of truth that would help me focus on my heavenly Father to inspire my children.

My Little Man

Elias is my second born. He took it upon himself to do the duties of the firstborn and be the man of the house until Dad came home. This nine-year-old boy wanted to be strong for his mom and sister.

I had to help him cope and understand it was okay to be the second born. Abigail's responsibilities were not his. He didn't have to put so much pressure on himself or try to control everything. I said, "If you're up to it and want to help, you can. I understand you want to protect us because that's the way God wired a man. That's great, but I'm your mom, and I am still in charge. You're not my husband to take over, because I know best."

He was traumatized from the accident, and we had to work through it. There were times he didn't want to talk or feel anything. I continued to talk and tell him, "I am here when you are ready." I made myself available and often spoke about Abigail to encourage them to share their feelings

Elias loves the Lord. He understands that when it is time, God will call us home. I told him, "God is not through with you, because it's a miracle you didn't have any injuries from the wreck. He has a plan for your life, and you are not done. Abigail did her duty here on earth, and she did a great job. Now, it's your turn." My son is growing up to be a strong man of God.

I See You, Baby Girl

Zoei is my third born. She was the baby of the house for some time and loved the attention, but things changed. Legend was born, and she was no longer the baby; now she's in the middle of two boys. Her big sister and best friend was gone. Daddy was her security blanket, and he wasn't around.

Sometimes, the middle child feels forgotten. She often did things to get my attention, like bother her brothers or repeat things over and over again in my face. I often looked in her eyes to let her know, "I see you and am here for you." Shortly after the accident, she started kindergarten. It took her some time to get in the swing of things at school.

She missed Abigail so much. She based some of her decisions on what Abigail liked. When it came time to pick a color for a particular item, she would say, "I pick green because that's Abigail's favorite color." It was her way to stay connected to Abigail.

In her heart, she somehow understood that Abigail was being cared for by Jesus and that she will see her again. We will spend eternity with Abigail. Until then, Zoei knows her big sister is watching over her.

Our Little Gift

Legend is my forth child. He is amazing. God sent him to us to help us love, smile, play, and laugh during our darkest time. He's our bundle of joy. Zoeí became his playmate. Elias had a little brother to watch over and is somewhat of a father figure for him.

Legend missed out on having Abigail in his life, but we often tell him about her and show him her pictures. He's now three and often points Abigail out in a picture. If he sees her, he will say, "That is my sister Abigail."

When Johnny came home, Legend often stared at him. It took him some time to get to know his papi. He watched how Zoeí and Elias treated their papi. They showed affection, respect, and how they played with their papi. Legend soon mimicked their actions. There would be times he sat on his papi's lap and fell asleep; it was like Johnny never left. We're very blessed to have Legend as part of our family.

This Is All a Process

It's going to take time to adjust to our new normal. Time doesn't heal you; it's what you allow God to do with the time that does. This was my time to run to Him and not away. He knows best and wants the best for me.

During this season, my love for the Lord increased drastically, and I learned to depend on Him in every way. We took each day as it came. We let go of things that weren't important and held on to what was. This helped us to set priorities and not to worry about petty things. This is the perspective God gave me.

Today, we're so much better. We still cry out of the blue, and I will continue to cry until I see Abigail again, but that's okay because the tears will come from a healed heart.

Chapter 5

Let's Fight

Fighting the Good Fight of Faith

I had to fight for Johnny; no one else was going to do it. No one else could believe like I could for him because God gave me the grace to do so.

Just three days later after the accident, doctors were thinking he was not going to make it through the night. This was the first of three times they predicted death for my husband. It didn't matter what the doctors said, because I had the promises of the Lord.

Shutting Down

Even though I had my Father's promises, I struggle at times to keep the hope. That Saturday, my husband was in a coma ... not alert or responsive.

He was on life support with so many tubes attached to his body.

All his organs were shutting down, except for his heart. It was beating slowly, close to a halt. The doctors advised me to call my family and friends to say their good-byes. My pastors did the same with the church family waiting outside. I was so afraid.

Later, the doctor asked, "Do you want us to resuscitate your husband if his heart stops?"

I said, "Of course; we are going to do everything in our power to keep him alive."

I don't want him to die. I love him. My children need their father.

Pastor Rob must have seen the distress in my eyes. He lovingly tried to prepare me for the worst. He said, "Ivette, this might be it."

I looked sternly at him and said, "No, Johnny is not going to die. I have promises of the Lord for our future, and they include Johnny."

He gently replied, "Some promises are for our future generation and not for us."

"Not mine. What the Lord has spoken to us includes Johnny. I know he's not going to die," I replied.

He empathetically said, "If that's what you believe, we are in agreement with you."

This is how I remember our conversation. It was assuring to know he believed with me.

Beauty in the Storm

Everything else seemed to be against me. I had to get away for a minute. I went to the bathroom in Johnny's room. I cried out to the Lord, "Lord, what is happening here? You told me that Johnny was going to live. Everything is going against that. Everything is shutting down." Feeling weak to hold on to hope, clearly I felt these words in my heart: "Who is in charge here? You or I? If it's I, you don't have to revive him. I told you, he is going to live. You have to fight." I realized it's not about them; it's about my faith. I had to believe God's promises no matter how bad it looked and stay out of God's way. I was recharged and left the room to speak to my husband's heart doctor. I knew what I had to do.

Crazy Faith

I found Johnny's doctor to say, "I want to change the orders. Do not revive him. He is going to live." *If he dies, then God will resurrect him.* By the look in his eyes, I speculated his thoughts were, *Poor Christian lady ... her daughter just passed away, she's pregnant, and has some kind of crazy faith.* Yes, that's me.

Later on, while waiting to see what would happen to Johnny, one of the nurses said, "I have never seen this before in all my years working in ICU. The heart doesn't usually last this long beating when every other organ is shutting down. This is like a battle."

Suddenly, I remembered a prophecy spoken over us many years ago. The visiting prophet said to Johnny, "There are three battles over your destiny. The last one will mark your life forever. I will do the impossible for the both of you." I felt even more encouraged.

I knew God was going to do the impossible. The waiting areas were packed with my family and church family. They were lining up two by two in the hallway, saying their good-byes to my husband as the doctors suggested, but their motivation changed. The pastors were believing with me. They told those lining up to pray over Johnny instead.

The support for Johnny was incredible. One doctor commented, "Who is this guy? There are so many people here just to see him." I was thankful for all these people coming to pray for my husband. As I was standing by Johnny's bed with Pastor Rob and his wife, in came our old friend and longtime pastor from years earlier, Pastor Sidney with his wife.

A Righteous Man's Prayer

Pastor Sidney asked, "How can we pray for Johnny?" Once I told him, he and his wife took turns in praying for my husband. I felt goose bumps.

There was something different about their prayers; it was intimate and ground shaking.

Pastor Sidney had known Johnny for over twenty years, since he was in the US Army. One part of his prayer still echoes in my head. With authority, he said, "Johnny, I hear that all you have to do is breathe. You are a soldier. I command you to breathe. You have a wife and kids to fight for."

The prayer continued like a drill sergeant commanding his soldier to follow orders. It was beautiful and powerful. One pastor commented, "Now that's the prayer of someone who knows Johnny as a dear friend."

Shortly after his prayer, Johnny's organs started to function. His levels were going up. *Thank God.* I went out to tell everyone with tears in my eyes, saying, "We're in the clear. Johnny's going to make it." I saw relief and joy from everyone.

I went over to Pastor Sidney and his wife to tell them their prayer was powerful. He replied, "He's not going to die. I know how it feels when the spirit of death is present. Johnny will get better."

I said, "Thank you."

It was getting late, and many had left. I stood through the night with my husband and my friend Candy in the waiting area. It was a long and miraculous day.

A Roller-Coaster Ride

We had our ups and downs. The doctors had nothing but bad reports to share. *Here they come again.* I felt guided not to really listen to them, but Pastor Rob and his wife listened for me. My husband had to endure a fourteen-hour surgery to repair his broken neck. Thankfully, some of our spiritual family waited by my side the whole time.

Every hour on the hour, the doctor called in giving us an update. I felt sick to my stomach each time the phone rang. *Did something go wrong? Is he okay?* Finally, I received the news that the surgery was a success.

There would be a couple of more scares on his condition throughout the week, but I knew he would not die. If he had been meant to die, then God would have taken him in the accident. There were three times when the doctors believed he would die, but each time, my God delivered him.

Speaking Life

Johnny was on life support and unconscious. The doctors would ask, "Do you want to unplug him? Do you want him to live this way for the rest of his life?"

I would answer affirmatively, "No, Johnny is in there. He will come back."

In one meeting, the doctors spoke negatively about his condition. I would immediately speak life to combat the negative. They would say, "He will be brain-dead."

I would say, "What if he does come back?" They would give me a positive response. I kept going. Johnny had a feeding tube. I would ask, "What if he gets better to eat normally?"

They would say, "If he gets better, we will remove the tube, and he will start eating honey-thick items. Then he will progress to nectar-thick items. Eventually, he will eat normally again."

Now they're speaking faith.

Don't ever doubt the power of speaking life. This is what I did over every bad report. I would ask for the healing process. Not only do you need to speak life over the negative, but you have to teach the ones involved to do the same. Trust in the Lord and His promises.

It's the Little Things That Helped

Johnny was unconscious, and I had to fight for him. When it came to the doctors' expert opinions on what to do with my husband, I felt alone. My family and friends were praying with me, but my husband was still not responding.

One day, I felt pressured from the doctors to unplug him, so I went to his room to pray over him. I asked him, "Johnny, can you hear me?" There would be no sound, but suddenly his eyebrow would go up and down. I felt relieved. *He can hear me.*

There was a time when his eyes and chest were swollen. His eyes were the size of golf balls. It was air trapped in his body causing him to swell up. If it didn't stop, the doctor was going to cut to release the pressure. Thankfully, it went down on its own.

Johnny doesn't remember any of this—not even moving his eyebrows when I asked if he could hear me. Now I jokingly say, "Your angel's job was to move your eyebrows whenever I asked a question." Those little things kept me moving forward. I knew he would get out of the coma.

Now We're Moving

One day, he came out of the coma and wanted the tube out of his mouth. His doctor approved a tracheostomy. It gave him the freedom to move his mouth, and he breathed through his throat. He didn't like it, but he was happy to move his mouth. They scheduled speech therapy to learn to speak with the breathing machine, but that would come in time.

Thank God for my sister Delia and her husband for staying with Johnny. We took turns to be with him. I would have the day shift, and they would take nights.

Beauty in the Storm

One evening, my sister Delia called to say that Johnny moved his left thumb to his index finger. I cried, "Thank you, Lord!" His healing was coming little by little.

Months later, my husband shared what had happened that night. This is what he said:

I was trying to grasp all that happened to me and my family. I was getting used to the nurse change times. This evening, I had a sweet elderly nurse. She would let me know when she would do my bed bath and would check on me often.

I would think about the morning routine with the doctor. He would check my hands and feet for response. He would say, "Squeeze my hand," but nothing happened. He would go to my feet and say, "Move your foot," but again, nothing. I felt disappointed with myself. I told my hands and feet to move, but they didn't respond. I could feel every touch, but I couldn't move.

While thinking on these things, my sister-in-law Delia came to spend time with me. She would share her day and things my kids would do when she watched them. Then she started to talk

> *about when her knee was injured and the therapy she did. She talked about how they applied pressure to the muscle and she would respond to the pressure.*
>
> *Then she held my left hand and applied gentle pressure. Once I felt the pressure, something inside me clicked. I signaled her to do it again. When she did, I squeezed back with my thumb. I was so happy. She was blown away and said, "Johnny, you squeezed my hand! Do it again." So I did. She took a video of it for my wife and called her. I signaled her to call the nurse.*
>
> *At first, the nurse thought it was just spasms, but when she saw I could do it on command, she said, "It's a miracle." Now, I couldn't wait to see my doctor's face in our morning routine.*

I agree with the nurse; this was a miracle.

Johnny developed a way to communicate with his eyes, besides blinking once for yes and twice for no. I would get my phone out and say the alphabet. Once I got to the right letter, he would blink a lot. Now I knew the common stuff like, "I am cold," "I'm in pain," and "Change the channel." This is how I found out about the double vision he was experiencing.

The doctor gave him a recommendation on how to treat it. It was a great feeling to communicate with my husband again.

It's Time to Tell Him

Father's Day was around the corner, and I was given a pass for Johnny to see the children. This would be the first time he would meet our newborn son, Legend. Before the children's visit, I wanted him to know about Abigail's passing away. His doctor said he was stable enough to hear about his daughter.

I couldn't do it alone. I asked Pastor Rob and his wife to be there with me. For weeks, I'd been carrying this burden of not telling Johnny about our daughter. My heart broke with the idea that he would not see her again on earth. He didn't get to say good-bye to her at the funeral. I didn't know how he would take it.

I arrived at the hospital to meet with Pastor Rob and his wife, Karen. She was there to support me, while her husband told Johnny. The night before, I tried to prepare my husband. I told him there was something very important I needed to tell him, and it wasn't good. He gave me a strange look. I told him, "I will tell you tomorrow, but you will need to prepare your heart. Remember, God's in control." I kissed him good-bye. I thought it was the best way to prepare him for the news.

Now I was at his bedroom door with my helpers. The nursing staff was on standby, just in case something went wrong. *Lord give me strength.* We stood around his bed, and Pastor Rob proceeded to tell him about what happen to Abigail. We were all in tears. He mouthed, "My baby, my baby," over and over again. His chest shook, trying to catch air from the depth of his tears for Abigail.

After a while, he stopped and looked at me. *Is he mad at me for waiting?* He mouthed, "Are you okay?" It dawned on him the terrible pain I'd gone through. He wanted to know how I was doing.

I cried, "I'm okay." He knew Abigail was more than fine. She was with the Lord. He was more concerned with me and my state of mind. My husband loves me so much. He understood why I'd waited, and he agreed it was a wise decision. This is the special bond we developed for over two decades.

Closure for Us

Daily, I would record myself telling Johnny about my day. It was my way to grieve. I described how beautiful Abigail looked for the funeral and all the funeral arrangements. He would hear my pain as I described my final moments with Abigail. I had to let

Beauty in the Storm

the pain out, and recording it for my husband was very therapeutic. Also, it was helpful to write this book.

When Johnny was ready to listen, he would not miss anything while he was away. I went as far to ask my church to record Abigail's funeral. I knew Johnny would love to see the way we said good-bye to our daughter. He decided to watch the video two months after his homecoming. One day, he said, "I'm ready to see Abigail's video." I quickly put on the disk. He wanted to be alone. I could hear him crying in the next room as it was playing. Once it was over, he looked peaceful.

He said, "I loved Pastor Jacob's message."

Pastor Jacob had said, "If Abigail can tell us anything from heaven, it would be these three things: it is amazing, it was worth it, and I am waiting for you."

"Abigail's waiting for me," Johnny said. There's peace in knowing that you will see your loved ones again and they're waiting to see you again. This gave him closure.

Keeping Hope Alive

Since the accident, the doctors saw the facts. My husband was in a terrible accident. He'd broken a main part of his neck, lost blood, and lost oxygen, and most of his organs had shut down.

This is why they thought he would be a vegetable, be paralyzed from the neck down, have many infections, eat through a tube for life, and need a machine to breathe for him for the rest of his life. Not many of us want to live this way. I get it. I don't blame them for asking me over and over again, "Do you want to stop life support? Do you want him to live this way?" I saw the facts, but I chose to believe God's truth.

I kept hold of God's promises for us. It took several months of therapy to see some outstanding progress, but immediately, Johnny could remember so much, even the events of the accident. He preached a message to the youth of our church for forty-five minutes without notes and all from memory. *It was so good.* Later, he helped edit this book using creativity and his typing skills.

You will see more of his progress as you continue to read about how he was able to breathe and eat regular food on his own. He developed strength and movement in his upper body by his routine stretching and exercising.

Finally, he learned to stand assisted. He's able to support weight on his legs for a small period of time. It will take crazy faith for Johnny to walk, but God is faithful. I believe that he will walk again. My miracle man will get his miracle.

CHAPTER 6

Rebuild

Leaving the Hospital

After a couple of months being in ICU, Johnny had to move to a nursing home for short-term care; this was where he began therapy. After much research and help from our friends, Johnny chose Trinity Neurologic Rehabilitation Center in Slidell, Louisiana, by blinking his eyes. He liked their name and reputation, and they had respiratory services for his breathing machine.

I'd hoped he would be home in couple of weeks after the accident, but his injuries were so severe that he needed care and therapy that I couldn't supply. The scariest part was not knowing how long it would be. It could take months or years depending on his progress and the amount of care he would need. Except for the times we were separated in the military, this would be the longest time we would be apart.

Arriving in Slidell

They were taking him away from me. That's how I felt when they said he need to leave the hospital. This meant I couldn't see him daily because he would be about three hours away. If there was an emergency, I couldn't be by his side. My heart was broken. *I miss him already.*

He would be transferred exactly two months after being in ICU at Our Lady of Lourdes Medical Center. I thank God we were not alone during this transition. The Lord gave us a special family to be by our side. They are the Amos family. Chris and Ronda felt in their hearts to spiritually adopt Johnny as their son.

When it came time to leave, I was in the ambulance with my husband. Chris wasn't able to come because he had to work, so Ronda drove behind us to Slidell with her adult children and my little daughter. My boys stayed with my best friend, Linda.

We arrived at the facility in the evening. My first impression was that the outside seemed nice, but inside it seemed bleak. *My goodness ... where am I leaving my husband? Is he going be fine here?* I would have thought otherwise if we arrived in the daytime.

There was long, white hallway, and all the doors were closed because most of the staff was gone for the day. Most of the patients were asleep, and some areas were dark. I was second-guessing our decision, but it was too late, and Johnny had to stay.

I was holding back my tears, and I kept my poker face on because I didn't want my sad face to be last thing he remembered. My husband is a family man. He'd rather be home with the family than anywhere else. It was definitely going to be hard for him.

Making Things Comfortable

The paramedics put Johnny in the bed near the window. It was a two-person room, but he had no roommate at the time. The bed faced a dresser for his clothes, and a nightstand was on the right. On the left side of the bed was his breathing machine. There was no television or radio for entertainment. *I hate to leave him here with nothing to do.* Ronda was thinking the same thing. She left and returned with a new television and paid for cable at the admin's office. We were very grateful.

The nurse came to assess Johnny's needs, and she didn't know he couldn't talk or move much. *Really? You didn't bother to read about your patient's condition?* This made me more uncomfortable about leaving him. After I told the nurse everything he could and couldn't do, she assured us that he would be checked on frequently.

Leaving Johnny Behind

It was getting late, and I needed to get home to my children. Johnny cried when we first arrived and again as we were getting ready to leave. Being unable to move or talk and stranded in a place away from your family can be overwhelming for anyone.

It was tough for me to leave him over 150 miles away, but this was his time. I remembered saying, "You were not there for me when Abigail passed away. You were not there when I gave birth to Legend. You were not there when we had her funeral. You were not there when I had to pack and move. You were not there when I cried myself to sleep. But Jesus ... Jesus was there with me. I'm not going to be here, but Jesus will be here with you. Now, it's your time to truly trust and depend only on God like I did the last two months." This was really hard for me to say, but I knew he needed to hear it. I knew my God was going to do something special with him. I hugged and kissed him good-bye. It would be a few months before he could come home again.

The Longest Ride

I held my little Zoeí close to me. So many thoughts ran through my mind. *When will I see him again? How will the children be without their father? When can he come home, and will he walk before he comes?* I had to let it go and let God take care of Johnny. After all, God loves him more than I ever will. "He's a child of God. A loving Father will always care for His son," I kept saying to myself. I thank God I didn't have to make the ride back home alone; it would not be safe to drive for such a long time feeling that way. Ronda and her family were there to help during this difficult time. I'm truly thankful for them.

Visiting Johnny

It took loads of planning to make a day's visit. Staying connected with both my husband and my children proved to be logistically challenging. I was very cautious leaving the newborn and my older children with the right person. I had to make sure my SUV was in good driving condition for the long trip. I needed funds for gas and food. And it was emotionally and physically draining coming back home.

Thankfully, the Lord provided the money through different channels, and my trusted friends watched my kids when my sister was unavailable. In the end, God worked it out for my good.

By His grace, I had the strength to make it through the day. Sometimes, I would take one of the older children to spend time with their father. It was important for them to stay connected with their papi as well.

I couldn't go many weekends, but Chris visited often when he worked in New Orleans. His wife, Ronda, and sometimes their children went on weekends when I couldn't make it.

Ronda cared for Johnny like her own son; it was something she felt in her heart to do. Johnny's birth mother wasn't always around when he was growing up. Ronda believed the Lord wanted her to fill this gap. She's been a mother to him ever since.

Johnny's Making Progress

After a few weeks in therapy, Johnny started having more movement in his hands. His first goal in therapy was to press the nurse's call button. At first, he could barely hold the button, but now he was able to push the button for help. This was exciting because he had more freedom to express a need.

He was talking better with the breathing machine. Since he was hours away, this gave us

Beauty in the Storm

more talk time over the phone to stay connected. We did not talk long because of the amount of energy it took him to breathe and speak. In time, he did get stronger.

I was seeing the hand of God moving. Johnny was gaining core strength to hold himself up. We would visit, and his hand would fall off the armrest sometimes. He would signal our daughter to lift his arm back up on the armrest. Zoei would think it was a game he was playing with her. Weeks later, he would lift it up on his own and sometimes trick Zoei to lift it up, but he did it himself before she got a chance. It was nice to see that my husband didn't lose his sense of humor.

With all his progress, there was one thing he was looking forward to do again beside walking: eating normally again. For months, his meals were vitamin and mineral milkshakes through his feeding tube. He missed chewing and tasting his food. The day he started soft foods and honey-thick liquids was exciting. Today, he savors every bite, never to take eating for granted. Little by little, he is coming back to me.

Depression Despite the Support

Johnny was blessed to be surrounded by so many amazing people. He had good days and bad days. He had uplifting physical therapists (PTs) and occupational therapists (OTs) that knew how to push him. These ladies were patient and encouraging. I just loved them.

Johnny's doctor was a Christian, and he would constantly pray with him. There was a respiratory therapist (RT) that would sing worship songs and talk to him about God to keep his spirits up while cleaning out his breathing tube. Johnny treasures these memories.

But when his birthday was drawing near, he was downhearted. He would say, "I don't want to celebrate my birthday." He told me not to bother to visit. I told him that I couldn't make it anyway because it was tough to get there on Mondays. I decide to surprise him and see if I could help lift his spirit. I knew exactly how to do it.

I arrived Monday morning to surprise him with a special gift. He was in therapy; I heard one therapist announce, "It's someone's birthday, and his name is Johnny." I walked in the therapy gym singing "Happy Birthday." In front of everyone, I held his gift in both hands: chocolate pudding with a single lit candle.

He started to cry as I came close to him to whisper, "Happy birthday."

He said, "I don't want to celebrate my birthday."

I replied, "Why not? You're given another year of life, and look at your progress."

He said, "Abigail didn't get to celebrate her birthday."

I replied, "That's where you're wrong. Abigail had the best birthday of her life. She celebrated with her heavenly Father." As I shared more, we both cried it out.

I could see his countenance begin to change. He cheered up and ate his pudding during lunch. Later, we laughed because the candle in the pudding brought back memories when we were dating. Years ago, we were going out for his birthday. While he was waiting in the car, I brought him a chocolate cupcake with a lit candle, singing "Happy Birthday." Memories like these help keep our relationship strong.

A November to Remember

This month was special for us because we celebrated our seventeen-year anniversary. It was also the month Johnny came home. He had so much progress. In fact, they were planning to teach me how to use and care for his breathing machine. Johnny was upset with the idea of coming home being attached to the machine. I told him that it didn't matter because I would care for him. This inspired him.

He told me and his RT, "In thirty days, I will get off this machine." His RT said she felt goose bumps when he declared it. They started to wean him off the machine. It took him two weeks, just before our anniversary. *That's my man.* I was so proud of him. He later said that he didn't think he needed the machine, but they made him believe he did. It's funny how when people mean well, they end up slowing your progress.

I went to visit him with some family for our anniversary. The nurse and their helpers were acting strange when I arrived. I heard them whisper, "Don't let her go over there." They told me, "Let's get Mr. Johnny out of bed into the wheelchair before you come into his room." *What's going on? Johnny doesn't mind me in the room when they are working.*

While we were waiting, we took the food that we'd brought to the dining area. When I entered the room, I was surprised with flowers, balloons, and a present. "Oh!" I exclaimed. I was touched that my honey went through all this trouble. The present was a nice, soft brown blanket. He said, "Since I can't hold you at night, the blanket will hold you and keep you warm until I can." Johnny has always been a romantic. Still today, I don't know how he paid for everything and who helped him to get it all.

Daddy's Home

It had been about six months since the accident, and the children missed their papi. His homecoming was around the corner. We made all the necessary arrangements to make the apartment functional. He was so much better, but he lacked the strength to use his arms. He arrived in a manual wheelchair because his legs were semi-paralyzed with very small movement. Once again, Pastor Scott and his wife were an enormous helped to get the home wheelchair-ready.

I had a list of supplies he needed and with the help of our community, church, family, and friends, we got it all. I felt ready until the reality hit. It proved we were still lacking, but with willing hearts, we would overcome.

The day came for Johnny's return. Our church rented a wheelchair-accessible van to ride back home in and use for the time being. Chris and Ronda helped with the drive home. Johnny was excited to finally get home. I didn't tell the children. I wanted to surprised them when they got home from school.

When they saw their dad, they cried and hugged him. Everyone was in tears—well, except for Legend. He was only seven months old. Johnny look forward getting to know his baby boy and fitting back into our daily lives.

CHAPTER 7

Be Still

Reality Hits

Johnny was home! We'd often spoken of this day over the phone, and now it was here. It was just a few days before Thanksgiving 2013. My church rented us a minivan made specifically for the disabled. We were able to travel to church and throughout the city as a family. Days before Christmas, Pastor Jacob announced from the pulpit the minivan was a Christmas gift to our family. This brought us to tears, and we could feel the love from the congregation as they cheered for us. I love my church. *It's great to have my family together again, especially for the holidays.*

Before Johnny came home from the rehab center in Slidell, the staff taught me how to care for him. We went over how to help him in and out of his chair and bed. The nurse said I had to give him shots every day. I nervously said, "I've never done this before."

She replied, "You will do great. Just pinch and stab the needle in one shot in his stomach."

This is not going to be too tough. I was so desperate to have my family together under the same roof that I underestimated all the challenges.

I was naive thinking it would be simple. When Johnny came home, he needed some help with eating and drinking. He had very limited movement in his hands, and his leg movements were mostly spasms. There was a feeding tube attached to his stomach; even though he wasn't using it, I had to keep it clean until the doctor removed it. Johnny was totally dependent on me.

I'd had little training and never took care of an adult in this manner before. Our first morning was a big reality check. It took me four hours to get Johnny ready for the morning. Afterward, I had to get my children ready, and finally I had time for myself. By the time I was done, I wanted to crawl back into my bed. *This is a lot tougher than I'd thought.* At night, I would change Legend's diaper and turn Johnny side to side in his bed to prevent bedsores. Needless to say, I didn't get much sleep. There were no nurses, aides, or anything; I had very little assistance. Delia would help me at times, but soon she moved out of state, and I would be on my own.

Time to Get Organized

I thought, *Jesus, what did I get myself into? What do You want me to learn from this? I am not learning anything, but I'm not giving up.* I love Johnny, and no one was going to take care of him better than I could. I was keeping my wedding vow; it was for better or for worse.

I tapped into my administrative skills to develop a routine and organize his medical supplies. Our master bathroom had more than enough cabinet space to put the majority of his supplies. In one corner, I placed all his daily items, and in the other side was all his nighttime stuff. In our bedroom, a table was set up to keep his bed items and bath supplies.

Now that the room was well equipped, we developed ways to get in and out of bed much more smoothly. It took a few months to get a system in place to make our life more bearable.

Better Together

This was becoming a living nightmare. I pushed myself to the limit until my body would hurt so badly. This lifestyle strained our marriage. Johnny and I would cry together while he hung from the body lift. We would feel sorry and upset for each other having to live this way.

If you'd met me, you would know that I am hardcore, as Zoei often tells me. Elias would say, "Mom, you're the glue of this house. You keep us together." *This glue is not going to give up.* I was determined to keep my family together. I continued to get better as time went on. It took almost six months for me to get stronger, faster, and more proficient.

My children were a great help. They would feed Johnny, change the TV channel for him, hold his phone while on a call, wash his hands, blow his nose, and clean his glasses. They also helped with Legend's feeding and diaper changes. We worked hard as a unit, and it grew us closer to each other.

My Revelation

One day, I received my answer from the Lord about my situation. I found that God wanted to teach me a couple of things before I had some help.

First, I had to let go and let God. I always try to control any situation to give me peace of mind. I found my peace by trusting that God had the day under control. If it took hours to get ready, then I was fine with it. I'd try to get better, but I wasn't going to be bitter. I knew in the end, all was well.

Secondly, I found strength that was deep within me. God had to take me past my comfort zone to

Beauty in the Storm

see what I had in my spirit. He wanted it to surface because others needed to see it. Others need to know that you can do anything; even when you're weak, you can be strong. Don't give up on God, because He will never give up on you. He will pull out your inner strength to show His greatness in you. I was ready for whatever was coming next.

Lastly, I learned to show love and acceptance to my husband. Johnny was an independent man. At first, he would not ask for help with things that I knew he needed. He had to know that he wasn't a burden. I would tell him it was okay to ask for help. He would say, "I don't want to be a burden."

I would reply, "I need you as much as you need me."

I could see the tears in his eyes, but later he was relieved. My service without complaining showed him love.

Johnny was disconnected, and he felt lost at home because he was gone for half the year, but I determined to change his and the children's mindsets. They had to learn their papi was back in charge. Before I did anything or went anywhere, I would ask his permission or opinion. If the children asked me for anything, I would tell them to ask their father first. Soon they realized this was how things worked in our household. This especially helped with Legend. He was the new kid, and he saw Papi was the head of the home. This boosted Johnny's confidence to lead again.

These lessons helped me to be a better wife and mother. When help arrived, I was in a different place in my life.

Getting Aid

Since Johnny was a veteran, he qualified for some assistance. The VA got us in touch with some local aid service. We took whatever we could get. They gave us fourteen hours a week to use for Johnny.

At first, we used two hours a night to put him in bed. The first agency was not very responsible. Sometimes a worker would come late or not at all, especially on the weekends. The agency seemed not to care. Thankfully, the VA gave us another agency that was more professional and attentive to our needs.

By this time, Johnny and I were pros, and we'd developed a system to make his care simple. We would train the aides in our method. Once they understood, our nights were smooth. They would tell Johnny, "You are a blessed man. Your wife is involved in your care; she has everything cleaned and organized for us." *Oh, he knows he's blessed.*

Some of the workers were like part of the family. And we were blessed to have some faithful and caring aides. It broke our hearts when it was time for them to move on. Opening our home to strangers and being vulnerable to them was something we didn't want to do constantly. Also, we had to retrain them.

A couple of years later, this changed. Delia felt in her heart it was time to return to Louisiana. She decided to be his permanent aide. I'm grateful for my sister wanting to help us. She's a blessing.

Our days were better than ever. It became clear that I needed help in the mornings more than in the evenings. It was difficult to get Johnny out of bed and take the children to school, and Legend started attending Mother's Day Out.

I took care of Johnny in the evenings, and Delia got him ready in the mornings. Johnny was dressed for the day by the time I came home from taking the children to school. This gave us more opportunity to enjoy our days.

Becoming Connected

My children and I mourned for a few months before Johnny came home. We overcame any bitterness and depression because we had one another to process our feelings. This was different for Johnny because he missed all of us equally. He only saw the children a few times at the hospital and the nursing home.

Once he was back with us, the reality of Abigail's death hit him hard. This was when he actually started to mourn for her. We saw a video of Abigail goofing around with her friend, and he started crying hysterically, saying continually, "I want her back." This was hard for me because I'd already been there and was in a better place now, but I decided to start over for him. We saw a recording of her funeral, talked more about our feelings, and cried together. This helped us both be on the same page.

We were adapting to our new normal. There were some terrible things we experienced that I can't even write in this book. Today, Johnny and I will laugh about the things that made us cry. We're determined to make it work.

Things were looking up. Johnny started outpatient therapy to increase his independence. The goal was for him to walk again. All we had to do was keep our eyes on the Lord, and He would do what He did best. He is God, not us.

The Amos Family

I'm thankful for the many days and nights when the Amos family came to our rescue. There were times when all my children were sick, and Chris took care of Johnny.

At other times, Ronda took me away to relax and recuperate. Regularly, both of our families dined together to unite us as one big family. They are my support system. I could not have done it without them.

We have many friends that helped us along the way. The Vasquez family is very grateful for them all. We saw God's love through their support. They are the hands and feet of Jesus.

Believing for a Home

Since we'd lost our home, we were believing for a new house. Every morning, I would pray with my children on the way to school. Our request to the Lord would mature over time.

At first we prayed, "God, we need a home to call our own. We know You will make it happen for us." It was a simple prayer for my children to grasp. After a while, they wanted to go deeper.

Then we dreamed of what we wanted inside and out. We thought of a few neighborhoods we wanted to live in. I had clippings of different decorations, colors, and furniture I would buy, with no limits. There had to be room for Johnny to maneuver in his wheelchair. I kept notes of everything we wanted for the house. We wanted clean, simple, and enough space for the things we really needed in the home. Our new perspective of life was "Less is *more*."

Lastly, we stopped asking and began thanking the Lord. We were praying for about a year. Around March 2015, I felt in my heart God has answered our petition even though we didn't have anything. It was a peace that surpassed my understanding.

2015 Arise Women's Conference

Every year, my church hosts a women's event called the Arise Women's Conference. They have great speakers from all over the world to inspire the two thousand–plus ladies in attendance. This year would be no different.

Before her death, Abigail looked forward to this event. We would take pictures at the photo booth, hang out with our friends, and grow spiritually together. I miss those times with my daughter.

About a month before the event, the church wanted their media team to do a video of me expressing what happened the day of the accident. They said if there was time, it would be displayed during the conference. I was excited to share my experience with those coming to the event.

That year's conference host was Pastor Eugene Reiszner. He is a lead pastor at one of our church's locations and one of our favorite pastors. The conference lasted for three days. I was anxiously waiting for the video to play on one of those days.

On the final day, I thought there were no time to play it. *Bummer. Either way, though, I had a blast.* But at the final hour, they said it was time to show a video of a woman that embraced her journey of faith; it was my video!

This was the first time I'd seen the final version with the audience. Once it was over, I was called to the front of the stage. *What's going on?* I was a hot mess because I'd cried so much during the video. Now I had to walk through a crowd of people cheering me on; it was so overwhelming. I sat next to my beautiful and loving pastor's wife, Michelle Aranza. She held me close as Pastor Eugene announced that I was the 2015 Arise Foundation Recipient. They presented me a mailbox, and then he said, "You know where a mailbox goes in front of? It's going in front of your ... brand-new house!" The place was electrified with cheers and tears. It was one of the best moments of my life.

This house was built in honor of Abigail and just for us. We would be the first ones to live in this fully furnished home. Everything on our prayer list was given except for two things. I realized they were not necessary because it would have added more time to clean and maintain. My heavenly Father is amazing! He knows the desires of my heart. No one knew what we were looking for in a home or the location we wanted to live in, but God knew, and that was enough.

There's power in writing down your vision, dreams, and prayers. Everything from the decoration to the location was ordained by God. Later, I was told they started to build it around March; that was around the time I felt to thank God for the answered prayer. I serve a great God.

They called the building of our home the Abigail Project. Manuel Builders took the lead, and Greg Manuel contacted many local builders who were interested in joining them on this mission. Time and materials were donated by the contractors and our local community. Builders who normally compete for work came together for the development of our home.

They specifically made the house handicap accessible with a roll-in shower, easy-access entrances, and large passageways to our bedroom. The design of the home was truly tailored to our needs with the look and feel that any family would love. We will forever be thankful for their generosity and compassion.

What's Next

In June 2015, we moved into our new home in a great location and the best schools around us. My children were able to get into the same charter school near our home.

Beauty in the Storm

Before the move, it took me over ninety minutes to drop off my children at different schools and return home. Now I would get home within thirty minutes. God gave me more time for myself and with my family. We have an awesome neighborhood. Everyone was so kind and brought us welcoming gifts. It was like the Lord was saying, "Welcome home."

Johnny started to practice standing. He went to therapy regularly through the VA support. He made so much progress. It took time, patience, love, and understanding to get us here. I can see the hand of God all over these past years. He has given me the desires of my heart, even down to the smallest things that no one knew about.

Now I'm asking, "What's next?" Everything is good. I have help with Johnny and my children. Our days are flowing very well. Johnny is way better than before he first came home. I'll tell you what's next. I need to be still and know that He is God. I am waiting for my miracle to see Johnny walking again.

I'm going to write more books. Now that's funny to me because I never dreamed of writing. Abigail was going to be the author of the house. She wrote many things, from poems to short stories. She passed the baton to her mama, and here I am writing our story for you.

I have done all I had to do for my family. Everything is working out. It is time for me to sit and be still and wait on my Father. The prophet said that God will do the impossible for the both us. I'm holding on to His promises.

Louisiana Is My Home

We're ready for whatever changes the Lord may bring, but in our hearts, Louisiana will always be our home. I have a confession: as a child, I did not like it here at all. My stepdad had military orders to move near Leesville, Louisiana. It was boring, and the humid weather was terrible. I planned to move to another state when I was older. This feeling didn't change after I was married.

Johnny and I lived in South Korea for over a year during his military tour. At first, he received orders to Fort Hood, Texas. We were excited to live in a big city and experience all it had to offer, but that was short-lived.

Since Johnny requested to stay longer in Korea, they changed his orders to Fort Polk, Louisiana. *Oh no! I don't want to go back there. At least we will be near my family, but soon Johnny will leave the army and move us to Lafayette.*

Living in Lafayette changed my perspective, but it took some time. There are some pretty amazing people here, like my friend Jackie. I said to her, "I

Beauty in the Storm

can't wait to move, because the Lord had called us to the nations."

She simply replied with a smile, "When you start to love Louisiana, that's when He will move you to your destiny." I'd never thought of it that way before, but she had a point.

Eight years after our conversation, I fell in love with the community in south Louisiana. The people here honestly care for each other. We have gone through some tough hurricanes and flooding. Each time, we rise up and help one another.

No one likes going through any storm that brings heavy devastation, but there's beauty in it. It comes from people who care so much for their neighbors to help ease the pain.

Recently, we went through a no-name storm with hurricane-like damages on August 12, 2016. Over forty thousand homes were flooded, and most lost everything they owned. Even we evacuated and moved four times trying to stay safe. Floodwaters came close to our home, but it stayed dry on the inside.

Once the waters receded, everyone went into action. My church checked on us to make sure we were fine. They quickly developed a system to help by gutting out homes, preparing meals, and providing supplies. All the area churches, schools, businesses, and the general public banded together to help their fellow man. This is the way it should be in every community in the world.

This is why I love it here. Even when I start to travel all over the world, I will always come back home to Louisiana. This is the place where I met and married Johnny; it is where I gave birth to all my children and where my daughter passed away. *I terribly miss her.* But it's my faith, my church family, and my community that helped me find the beauty ... the beauty in the storm.

Abigail's Poem

This is the poem that slipped out of my prayer journal. In honor of my daughter, I didn't make any corrections to it. I pray it will bless you the way it blessed me.

BE LIKE THE TREE
by Abigail Vasquez

I want to be like a tree, where my roots grow down deep. I can never be pulled out of the ground and sold. Therefore, I must be planted with faith, kindness, love (ect.), so that I may grow strong in you; so I may have everlasting life. During the storms of life, I may bend, but I will surely not break, for you allowed these storms to come so I may become stronger, and wiser, and my roots will grow down deeper in you. When the enemy comes, I know that NO WEAPON FORMED AGAINST ME WILL PROSPER. The reason you said we would flourish like trees, is because you knew we would

Ivette Vasquez

go through difficult times. With you on my side I learned that nothing can hold me back. In the end I want to grow beautiful fruits, to show that you are beautiful in me.

Family Photos

We were married November 17, 1996

Our Sweet Abigail

Christmas 2012 Our last family photo
with Abigail and Legend in my belly

Our 17th Wedding Anniversary at the nursing home in Slidell

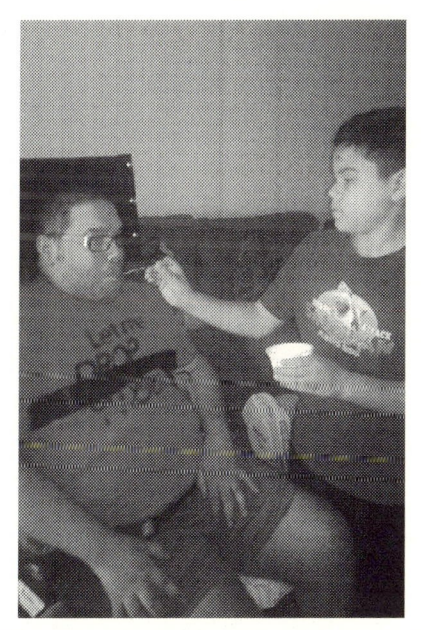

Elias helping to feed his dad

Zoeí pushes her dad around

Chris and Ronda Amos with us

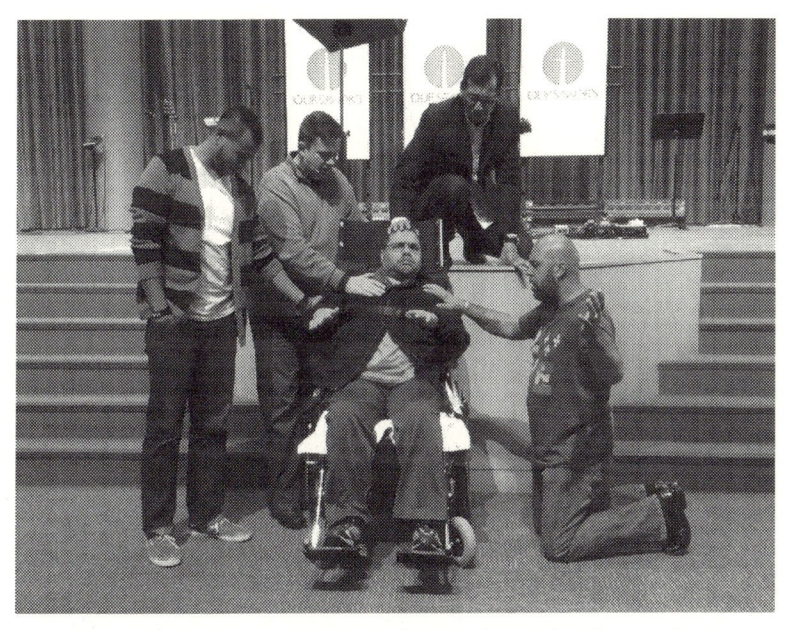

Johnny's first day back to church Nov 2013

First day in our new home June 12, 2015

Our family picture taken on
Independence Day 2016

Afterword

I don't know what challenges you are facing, but I know it doesn't need to swallow you up. During the hardest moments of my life, I found hope. I didn't give up, because I chose to trust in God. You have to believe this is not the end—because it's not.

Life will move forward. You have to believe in the kindness of people who will give you a shoulder to cry on. You have to believe that God has a plan for you. Time doesn't heal you; it's what you allow God to do with the time. Embrace your journey, and it will bring healing.

I made the decision in my youth to know God, and I couldn't make it this far in life without Him. Give up trying to make it on your own and surrender your life to God. Give up trying to be a loner and build true loving relationships.

We were never meant to live this life on our own. Find a good Bible-believing church, and get to know other Christians to help you grow in faith. Don't just show up to church; get involved to impact your community. I don't know where

I would be without the support of my spiritual family and community.

Today, I encourage you to get to know God in an intimate way. God understands our pain because His Son, Jesus, died for us on the cross. Through His death, the penalty of sin was paid in full. Sin separates us from God, but we are able to draw close to Him through Jesus. I encourage you to accept Him as your savior and Lord.

Repeat this prayer:

Dear heavenly Father, I want to know You more in an intimate way. I ask You to forgive me of my sins. I surrender my life to You. Let Your Holy Spirit abide in my heart. Thank You for the sacrifice Jesus made for me. In Jesus's name, amen.

Acknowledgments

First, I would like to thank my heavenly Father for showing me the beauty in the storm. He's been with me through this journey of grief. His dreams are big for me. I am aware that it's not me but Christ in me. By the grace of God, I am what I am.

To my loving husband, Johnny, I will never leave your side, and we will continue to fight together against the odds. I believe in you and us. You have been very instrumental in the putting this book together, and I look forward to the many projects we will work on.

A special thank-you to my children. Elias, I'm proud of the man you are becoming. Zoeí, you're my little princess and prayer warrior. Legend, you gave me the extra strength and joy I needed in my life. You are all an amazing crew. I love being your mom.

I am truly grateful to those who helped me with this book—to all who supported me, talked things over, read, allowed me to quote their remarks, assisted in proofreading, and have been with me over the years.

Thanks to my church, OSC, and our community for being the hands and feet of Jesus through our trials and tribulations.

Please Share

You are invited to share *Beauty in the Storm.*

- Give this book as a gift to your family and friends.
- Let us know how this story changed you.
- Reach out to those in need by providing copies of the book to people that need encouragement and inspiration.
- Your organization can request the author as a speaker.
- Consider setting up a group to meet to discuss the book.

Keep up with us by visiting my Instagram page, our Facebook page, and our website for updates on Johnny's progress and other upcoming books.

Social media:
- instagram.com/s.ivette.vasquez
- facebook.com/AbigailMyHero.Org

For more information, visit abigailmyhero.org.

Printed in the United States
By Bookmasters